I0481275

Bitcoin Trading with Paxful

What I wish I knew when I started trading

By Elvis Nyakangi

Bitcoin Trading With Paxful

Notice of Rights

Notice of Liability

Trademark Notice

TABLE OF CONTENTS

Target Audience

This book is aimed at beginner Bitcoin traders and researchers looking to understand how Paxful works.

The book is divided into two main sections.

In the first section, you will learn about the basics of Bitcoin.

In the second section, you will learn about Paxful and how to use it for Bitcoin trading.

Disclaimer

This book is written only for information purposes. Please be aware that the price of Bitcoin fluctuates so much and relies more on speculations. There is no existing data that you can use to tell whether the price of Bitcoin will go up or down the next day.

Bitcoin Glossary

Altcoin: Means any other Cryptocurrency other than Bitcoin.

Anti-Money Laundering (AML): Means laws that regulate how people acquire and distribute money through financial institutions to prevent money laundering. Money Laundering is the process of converting money earned illegally to clean money (legal money).

Arbitrage: Is the buying of assets in one market and selling them in a different market at a profit.

ASIC (An application-specific integrated circuit): This is a device that is used to mine digital currency.

Bitcoin address: This is a mixture of letters and numbers that is between 26 to 35 characters long that are used for receiving Bitcoin payments. It is like your bank account number.

Bitcoin Faucet: This means being rewarded in Bitcoins for performing certain tasks for instance, completing surveys or clicking ads.

Bitcoin Wallet: This is an application that is used to send, receive, and store Bitcoins. Bitcoin wallets interface with the Bitcoin Blockchain.

Blockchain Hash ID: This is an ID that is assigned to every verified and completed Bitcoin transaction. It is like a paid invoice number. You can use websites like https://bch.btc.com or https://xrpscan.com to search for your Hash ID if asked for one by your bank.

BlockChain: It is a network of records linked to each other or a network of cryptocurrency transactions.

BTC: Is the abbreviation of Bitcoin

Cloud mining: This is the process of mining Bitcoins using a cloud network infrastructure. This means you will not be using your computer's power to mine.

Coin Exchange: It is a platform where you can buy and sell Bitcoins.

Crypto Jacking: This is hacking and then using of someone else's computer to mine cryptocurrency without their permission.

Cryptocurrency: A digital currency that relies on cryptography to validate transactions, removing the need to have a trusted central authority.

Escrow: This is a 3rd party system that holds money and disburses it from the 1st Party to the 2nd party after all transaction agreements have been met. For instance, if you are a Bitcoin seller on Paxful and you've got a buyer, you will release your Bitcoins to Paxful Escrow. Once you confirm that you have received the payments, Paxful will release the Bitcoins from its escrow to the buyer.

Fish or Minnow: A person who has small amounts of cryptocurrency assets.

Halving: Bitcoin halving is a moment when mined Bitcoins are cut in half (50%).

Hardware Wallet: This is a device that is used to store cryptocurrency.

Hashrate: This is the measuring unit of the processing power of a device in the Bitcoin network. A hash rate of 10 Th/s means the device makes 10 trillion calculations per second. A higher hash rate means more competition because more resources are required to attain the hash rate.

KYC (Know Your Customer): It is the process of verifying who your customer is by asking him/her to share identifying information like ID, address, email, etc. to mitigate risk.

Ledger: In cryptocurrency, a ledger is a record of all transactions that have occurred. For instance, a record of Bitcoin transactions.

Miners: People involved in the process of mining Bitcoins.

Mooning: This means a rapid and sharp rise in price or value.

Protocol: This is a set of rules of how Bitcoin works.

Satoshi or SATS: Means the smallest unit of Bitcoin equivalent to 0.00000001 BTC (100 millionth of a Bitcoin).

TH/s: Means tera hashes per second.

Virtual Currency: This is a type of digital currency that is held within a blockchain network.

Understanding Bitcoin

Introduction

Bitcoin is the name assigned to one of the most popular and the largest Cryptocurrency in existence. The genius behind this currency has chosen to be a mystery to many.

Will Bitcoin be strangled to death by central governments, or will it eventually crash and die? Or will it remain as a currency that keeps rising and falling without being embraced by central governments as one of the mediums of exchange? The answer to these questions remain as unknown as the founder of Bitcoin.

For now, let us dive into the basics of Bitcoin and later Paxful.

What is Bitcoin?

In simple terms, Bitcoin is an electronic payment system or virtual currency that is not controlled by any person, financial company, or government. Just like real money, Bitcoin is stored in secure wallets.

Anyone can create Bitcoins through a process called Bitcoin mining that we will explain later.

A Brief History of Bitcoin

Bitcoin is believed to have been invented by Satoshi Nakamoto in January 2009. To this day, Satoshi remains anonymous, and nobody knows who he or she is.

- **18th August 2008**: Bitcoin.org, the largest Bitcoin resource website is born.
- **October 31, 2008**: Satoshi Nakamoto publishes a white paper about Bitcoin: A Peer-to-Peer Electronic Cash System.
- **January 9, 2009**: Version 0.1 of Bitcoin is released with a system that would create a total of 21 million Bitcoins.
- **January 12, 2009**: The first transaction of Bitcoin currency took place between Satoshi and Hal Finney, a renowned cryptographer.

Is Bitcoin legal?

The answer as to whether Bitcoin is legal or illegal varies from state to state and country to country. Some countries have laws that define the usage of Bitcoin by their Citizens while others do not have any laws at all (are neutral). The percentage of those that do not have any laws on the usage of Bitcoin is higher than those that have.

Some of those countries that have laws prohibiting the use of Bitcoins as of February 2021 includes:

- **Algeria**: Selling of Buying Bitcoin is prohibited in Algeria.
- **Egypt**: Has a religious decree classifying commercial transactions in Bitcoin as haram (prohibited under Islamic law).
- **Nigeria**: On 5 February 2021, The Central Bank of Nigeria issued a circular informing financial institutions that cryptocurrency exchange is prohibited, and accounts of users found operating cryptocurrency exchanges should be closed immediately.
- **Bolivia**: The Central Bank of Bolivia issued a resolution banning Bitcoin and any other currency not regulated by a country or economic zone in 2014.

- **Nepal**: On 13 August 2017, Nepal Rastra Bank declared Bitcoin illegal.

Read more about the updated list of **The Legality of Bitcoin use per Country or territory**: (https://en.wikipedia.org/wiki/Legality_of_bitcoin_by_country_or_territory)

Bitcoin Mining

When you first heard of Bitcoin mining you might have thought of something closer to digging the ground to mine coins. But that is not the case. Bitcoin is intangible.

Bitcoin mining involves a process of maintaining the blockchain by adding new and validated blocks to it. The miners are then rewarded with Bitcoins and transaction fees.

To mine Bitcoins, you need internet access (to sync the block), a power supply, a mining computer (hardware), and mining software (to connect to the blockchain).

Bitcoin Mining Hardware

8 years ago, it was easy to mine Bitcoins at home. It only required a slightly powerful computer and a steady supply of power. As Bitcoin mining started becoming popular, miners started using computers with more computational power to mine. It became increasingly difficult for small miners to keep up at that scale as such types of computers flooded the network with fresh hash rates. The increase in hash rates meant more competition and lower rates.

(Here is a live Total Hash Rate chart of the estimated number of terahashes per second the Bitcoin network is performing in the last 24 hours: https://www.blockchain.com/charts/hash-rate)

Despite the low-profit margins, some small miners continue to thrive in the industry because of the rise in Bitcoin price. If you are a small miner and want to make some reasonable profit with Bitcoin mining, then we recommend that you use the Bitmain Antminer S19 Pro that costs $10,000 (as of February 2021) to create your small mining farm or a pool of several graphic adapters. Bitmain Antminer S19 Pro has a maximum hash rate of 110TH/s for a power consumption of 3250W.

With a dollar to Bitcoin exchange rate of 1 BTC=$34.871.2, one Antminer S19 Pro can mine about 0.2789 Bitcoins per year which is about $9,727.82.

The electricity bill will cost about $3,369.60 per year to mine 0.2789 Bitcoins.

This means that your profit is about $6,358.22 (per year). This is quite some decent amount earning in a year.

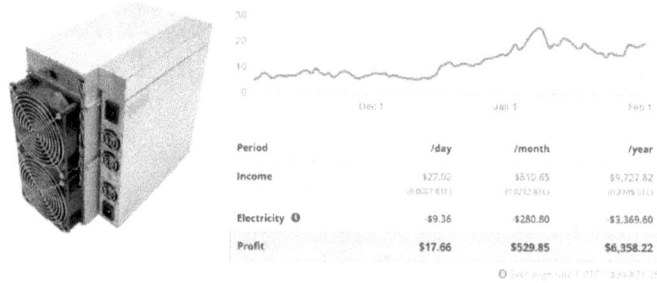

Period	/day	/month	/year
Income	$27.02	$810.65	$9,727.82
	(0.0007 BTC)	(0.0232 BTC)	(0.2789 BTC)
Electricity ⓘ	-$9.36	-$280.80	-$3,369.60
Profit	$17.66	$529.85	$6,358.22

ⓘ Exchange rate 1 BTC = $34,871.15

Bitmain Antminer S19 Pro (110Th)

Photo 1: Bitcoin mining with Antminer s19 Pro cost estimates/Photo source asicminervalue.com

Bitcoin Mining Software

Other than hardware, you also need to install Bitcoin mining software. The mining software is used to connect your mining hardware to the Bitcoin mining network or Blockchain. A mining software can also be used to show your mining stats, temperature, and control input and output.

There are hundreds of paid and free mining software. Some of the most popular ones include:

- **CGMiner**: One of the most used open-source cryptocurrency mining software compatible with operating systems like Windows, OS X (macOS), and Linux. It can be used with GPU, FPGA, and ASIC hardware. It can be used for solo mining or multipool mining.
- **Awesome Miner**: Awesome Miner is a Windows application for managing and monitoring mining of Bitcoin, Ethereum, Litecoin, and other cryptocurrencies. Awesome Miner provides centralized management for up to 200,000 miners from a single user interface. All popular ASIC miners are supported and all popular GPU and CPU mining software are also supported. It has free and paid versions

- **BFGMiner**: Is a free multi-threaded, multi-blockchain, multi-pool ASIC, FPGA, GPU, and CPU miner with dynamic clocking, monitoring, and fanspeed support for bitcoin
- **MultiMiner**: Is a graphical application for cryptocurrency mining on Windows, OS X, and Linux. MultiMiner simplifies switching individual devices (GPUs, ASICs, FPGAs) between crypto-currencies such as Bitcoin and Litecoin. Most reviews on TrustPilot indicate that they are not trustworthy. Be sure to do your background research about MultiMiner before using it.

This far, you will have noticed that the entire process of mining Bitcoins is complex and requires substantial capital. Neither your home laptop nor a smartphone can help you be a profitable miner. They are ineffective. Therefore, the only best option left if you do not have enough capital to invest in devices with powerful computational power is to use peer-to-peer Bitcoin trading marketplaces.

In such platforms, you do not mine Bitcoins but buy and sell Bitcoin when its value appreciates just like it happens in forex trading (trading of currencies).

Paxful is one of the recommended Bitcoin trading marketplaces that we will be discussing in this book in the next chapter.

Photo 2: Bitcoin Mining Warehouse/Photo by Stefen Chow

Other forms of getting Bitcoins

Other than mining Bitcoins, you can also get Bitcoins through micro earnings, affiliate, Bitcoin trading, and exchanges.

- **Micro Earnings**: This involves performing tasks and getting paid in form of Bitcoins. For example, being paid in Bitcoins to click ads, take surveys, etc. This method of getting Bitcoins is risk-free but the returns are low. Examples of websites that pay in Bitcoins to click on ads include btcclicks.com, coinbulb.com, bitclix.io, etc.
- **Affiliate Program**: You can share a link of any peer-to-peer Bitcoin exchange platforms

or Bitcoin marketplaces like Paxful, Localbitcoins, CoinMama, etc. in your blog posts or social media and get paid for any person who buys Bitcoins through your affiliate link. Reliable Bitcoin marketplaces that offer affiliate programs include LocalBitcoins, Paxful, Coinbase, Coinhouse, Bitpanda, Coinmama, Binance, etc. This method is risk-free but the returns depend on how many traders you can refer.

- **Trading**: This involves buying Bitcoin when its price is low and selling when its price is highest. This method entails very high risk but has the potential of high returns.
- **Exchanges**: This method involves getting Bitcoins through exchanging with goods and services like Gift Cards, Gold, game items, card, etc.

Bitcoin Use Case

The number of companies that accept Bitcoins as a form of Payment is slowly growing with Apple being the latest fortune 100 company that has announced that they will begin accepting Bitcoins as a form of payment.

Below are the three most common uses of Bitcoin.

- **Cross-border Payment**: You can send payments in form of Bitcoins to any person in any country in the world without the need of a bank.
- **Source of Income:** Bitcoin trading can act as the main source of income. How it works is that you buy bitcoins when the price is low and sell when it is higher. You can also invest in mining Bitcoins and selling them in exchange for real currency.
- **Shopping online**: You can shop online using Bitcoins. Some of the most reputable companies that allow Bitcoins include Overstock.com, AT&T, Microsoft Xbox stores, Newegg, BMW dealerships, Express VPN, Shopify, NordVPN, Rakuten, Bitrefill, Reddit, PayPal, **Apple Pay,** etc.

Bitcoin Rates

The price of Bitcoin is unpredictable. It can increase or decrease steadily over a short period. Therefore, Bitcoin should be seen as a high-risk asset, and you should never store money that you cannot afford to lose.

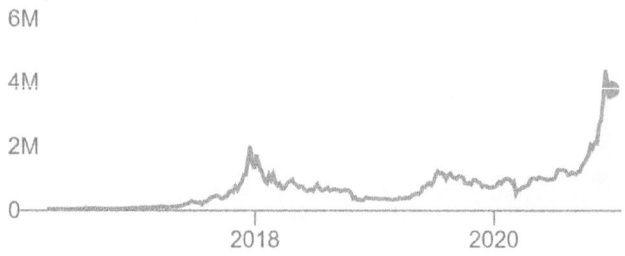

Photo 3: 5 years Bitcoin fluctuation against the US (United States) dollar

Bitcoins can be converted to any currency using Bitcoin exchange platforms like Paxful and withdrawn to your bank account, online wallets like Skrill, PayPal, WeChat Pay, Zelle Pay, PayU, or mobile money service providers like Mpesa or Airtel money.

Bitcoin Taxes

Bitcoin taxes vary from one country to another. Some countries do not charge Tax on Cryptocurrency trades while others do.

In the US, the sale or exchange of convertible virtual currency (Bitcoin included), or the use of convertible virtual currency to pay for goods or services in a real-world economy transaction, has tax consequences that may result in a tax liability. For federal tax purposes, virtual currency is treated as property. General tax principles applicable to property transactions apply to transactions using virtual currency.

For U.S. tax purposes, transactions using virtual currency must be reported in U.S. dollars. Therefore, taxpayers will be required to determine the fair market value of the virtual currency in U.S. dollars as of the date of payment or receipt. If a virtual currency is listed on an exchange and the exchange rate is established by market supply and demand, the fair market value of the virtual currency is determined by converting the virtual currency into U.S. dollars (or into another real currency which in turn can be converted into U.S. dollars) at the exchange rate, in a reasonable manner that is consistently applied.

You will however not be taxed if you donate Bitcoins to a tax-exempt charity or non-profit, buying Bitcoin with cash and holding, transferring Bitcoin from one wallet to another, and transferring Bitcoins between Paxful account or from an external wallet to Paxful account.

If you are not in the US and are a Bitcoin trader then you will need to consult your tax agent or representative on whether you are required to pay withholding tax, include it in income tax, or any other form of tax in your country.

Process of Filing Bitcoin Taxes

To file your sales taxes in the US, you are required to report gains on form 8949. Tax gain ranges from 0% to 37% depending on your annual income. You will need all the transaction invoices to properly file your taxes. You can use https://www.cointracker.io to track all your sales. You can connect your exchanges and wallets with CoinTracker to automatically track your crypto performances and taxes.

Paxful Overview

What is Paxful?

Paxful is one of the leading Bitcoin peer-to-peer Trading Marketplaces. Paxful can be used to hold, convert, transfer, buy and sell Bitcoins using a wide variety of available payment methods and currencies.

Company Profile

Paxful, Inc. was founded in July 2015 by Ray Youssef (CEO) and Artur Schaback (CPO). Paxful started as a platform for selling Gift Cards in exchange for Bitcoins and grew to become one of the largest peer-to-peer Bitcoin trading marketplaces. According to Paxful CEO Rat Youssef, Paxful does over 40 million USD a week in trade volume and over 60,000 trades a day.

The name Paxful comes from the word "Pax" which in Latin means Peace. The founders of the company used the word Pax to name their company because they believed that Bitcoin promised a more peaceful world.

Paxful.com is available in 21 languages with over 300 payment methods.

Its headquarters is in New York, United States.

Services Offered by Paxful

Some of the services offered on Paxful.com include:

- Buying and Selling Bitcoins
- **Paxful Affiliate program**: This is a program where you get paid 50% of the escrow fee if the people you invite to Paxful make a successful trade. Any person can join Paxful affiliate program.
- **Paxful Peer Program**: These are Paxful users that spread the word about Paxful to crypto enthusiasts and are in return paid $5 for every new referral in addition to the affiliate commissions.
- **Paxful Kiosk**: This is a form that you are supposed to embed in your website or blog.

People can use the form to initiate Bitcoin transactions. You will earn affiliate commissions for each successful trade originating from your form. Below is a photo of how the form looks like in action.

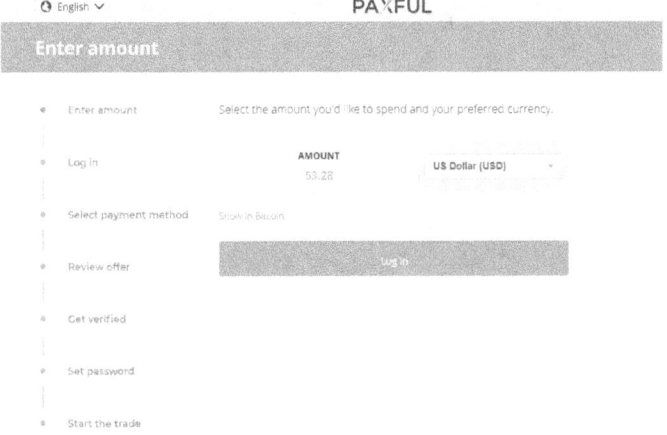

Photo 4: Example of Bitcoin Kiosk form

Creating a Paxful Account

Paxful is open for use for any person who is 18 years and older, with a valid National ID or passport, and who is in any country other than US OFAC banned countries below. To create a Paxful account follow the procedure below:

1. Go to **https://paxful.com**
2. Click Get Started and the Create Account (at the top menu)
3. Enter your email and Password then click Create Account button
4. Verify and confirm your email
5. You are done with creating your account. You will immediately be assigned a wallet.

Paxful Account Security Measures

If you have read online reviews about Paxful on forums, or social media sites, you will notice that some people have had their accounts breached. At the end of this book, we will highlight about some of the common scams and precautions that you should take to avoid being scammed.

For now, let us look at some of the security measures that you should take and observe to protect your account from being breached

- **Do not click on links that take you out of Paxful platform**: Some of those links might redirect you to sites that automatically download malware to your browser or device, or the link might take you to a fake website that looks like Paxful or your bank and trick you to give sensitive information. Within minutes, your Bitcoins will be stolen, or your bank account will be drained.
- **Do not share personal information in trade chats**: Even if you trust people you are trading with, do not share personal information in chats because if a data breach occurs on Paxful.com, hackers will have access to your information.

- **Setup Two-factor authentication by visiting your account settings:** Two-factor authentication (2FA) is a two-step verification method. It is an additional layer of security. If a hacker manages to get your password, he or she will also need to access your phone number to receive a login verification code or QR Code.
- Create strong passwords and unique passwords. Do not use passwords that you have used on other platforms.
- Do not share your email address with anyone as scammers/hackers can use it to send phishing links.
- Make sure your computer has a reputable antivirus to stop malware installation

Why Paxful accounts are suspended

Before we explain to you why your account was banned or suspended, below is a definition of what it means to be suspended, locked, frozen, oh-hold, and banned.

Locked (reversible): This may be due to suspicious access of your account. The account is locked to protect it. Check your email inbox and click the unlock link to unlock your account. Ensure that you are accessing your account from your account specified location/country.

On-hold (reversible): Once your account has been put on hold, you cannot use it for any transaction until a review of your account by Paxful team is completed. After the review is complete, you will be asked to verify your identity.

Frozen: You cannot temporarily buy, sell, or transfer funds on Paxful until your frozen period expires.

Suspended (not reversible): You cannot use your Paxful account until when your suspension is lifted by Paxful. Accounts are normally suspended for one year. If you fail to resolve a dispute or problem that led to account suspension within one year, then your account might be permanently suspended.

Banned (not reversible): You are permanently restricted from using Paxful for any activity. You can however login once and move your funds to an external wallet.

Some of the reasons as to why your account is banned or suspended include.

- Conducting or asking for trade to be done outside Paxful
- Making bank chargebacks or PayPal reversal without Paxful permission
- Selling of used or redeemed gift cards
- Opening multiple Paxful accounts
- Providing false profile verification documents
- Accessing Paxful with a VPN
- Accessing Paxful from OFAC banned countries
- Your account will be banned if you create another account after being previously suspended
- **External links**: Do not share external website links in chat, unless it is for payment purposes, and in such case, the external website link should be indicated in your offer terms. The external website link should also not direct users to a page that contains your contact details
- **Reselling Gift cards**: You should not buy gift cards from another vendor and sell them on Paxful. You are only allowed to sell gift cards that you have purchased.
- Do not pay with a bank account not registered under your name. If a dispute arises, you will be on the wrong side of the law and your account will be suspended.

- Do not trade with a trader **from OFAC banned countries**. If you do so, then you are all guilty and your accounts will be banned.

Paxful Fees

Paxful does not charge any fee for buying cryptocurrencies on its platform. However, it charges the following fees for selling cryptocurrencies.

Payment Type	Selling Cryptocurrency
Bank Transfers	0.5%
Credit/Debit cards	1%
Digital Currencies	1%
Online Wallets	1%
Cash	1%
Goods and services	1%
Gift Cards	3% for all types of Gift Cards. 5% for iTunes and Google Play Cards

External wallets fees

For sending cryptocurrency to external wallets like Coinbase, Paxful charges the following fees.

- $0 - $9.99 = 0.00008 BTC
- $10 - $19.99 = 0.00016 BTC
- $20+ = 0.0004 BTC

Internal Wallets

For sending Bitcoin to an internal wallet like from one Paxful wallet to another Paxful wallet, Paxful charges the following fees if you exceed 5 free internal sends per month.

- $1.00 or 1% of the amount being sent, whichever is greater

Paxful Payment Methods

Paxful has over 300 payment methods which include Bank Transfers (9 available choices), Online Wallets (169 available choices), Gift Cards (124 available choices), Cash Payment (18 available choices), Debit/Credit cards (20 available choices), Digital Goods (20 choices) and Goods and services (4 choices).

The most popular payment methods on Paxful include:

Bank Transfers

- ✓ Bank Transfer
- ✓ Domestic Wire Transfer
- ✓ Faster Payment System (FPS)
- ✓ IMPS Transfer
- ✓ International Wire Transfer (SWIFT)
- ✓ UPI Transfer

Online Wallets

- ✓ WeChat Pay
- ✓ M-Pesa
- ✓ PayPal
- ✓ Cash App
- ✓ Zelle Pay
- ✓ Google Pay

Gift Cards

- ✓ Amazon Gift Card
- ✓ Steam Wallet Gift Card
- ✓ Google Play Gift Card
- ✓ eBay Gift Card
- ✓ iTunes Gift Card
- ✓ OneVanilla VISA/MasterCard Gift Card

Cash Payments

- ✓ Western Union
- ✓ Vodafone cash payment
- ✓ Cardless cash
- ✓ Cash Deposit to Bank
- ✓ MoneyGram
- ✓ OXXO

Debit/Credit Cards

- ✓ Walmart MoneyCard
- ✓ GreenDot Card
- ✓ Paysafecard
- ✓ Bluebird American Express
- ✓ MyVanilla Prepaid Card
- ✓ Visa Debit/Credit Card

Digital Currencies

- ✓ Tether USDT
- ✓ Ethereum ETH
- ✓ Litecoin LTC
- ✓ TRON TRX
- ✓ Bitcoin Cash BCC/BCH
- ✓ Stellar Lumens XML

Paxful Verifications and limits

Paxful has a Know Your Customer (KYC) policy where traders who exceed a trade of $10,000 are required to verify their identification by submitting their National ID and proof of address.

Below is a list of the four Levels of Paxful Verification and the time it takes.

Level			Time it takes
1	Email and Phone	$1000	Instant (automated)
2	ID	$10,000	Instant (automated)
3	Address	$50,000	24 hours (automated)
4	Enhanced due diligence	$50,000+	25 hours (Automated)

NOTE 1: Automated verifications take up to 24 hours. If you have not received an answer within 24 hours, it means that your document is going through manual verification which takes between 2 to 7 days.

NOTE 2: In some cases, verification of documents may fail if you provide false identification, operate more than one Paxful account, fail to provide required documents, are connected to illegal activities, etc.

NOTE 3: Since November 2020, ID verification became mandatory for citizens in the following countries

1. American Samoa (USA)

2. Andorra

3. Anguilla (UK)

4. Antigua and Barbuda

5. Argentina

6. Armenia

7. Aruba (Netherlands)

8. Australia

9. Azerbaijan

10. Bahamas

11. Barbados

12. Belize

13. Bermuda (UK)

14. Bolivia

15. Brazil

16. British Virgin Islands (UK)

17. Cayman Islands (UK)

18. Chile

19. Colombia

20. Cook Islands (New Zealand)

21. Costa Rica

22. Curacao (Netherlands)

23. Dominica

24. Dominican Republic

25. Ecuador

26. El Salvador

27. Falkland Islands (UK)

28. Faroe Islands (Denmark)

29. Fiji

30. French Guiana (France)

31. French Polynesia (France)

32. Georgia

33. Gibraltar (UK)

34. Greenland (Denmark)

35. Grenada

36. Guam (USA)

37. Guatemala

38. Guernsey (UK)

39. Guyana

40. Haiti

41. Honduras

42. Iceland

43. Isle of Man (UK)

44. Jamaica

45. Jersey (UK)

46. Liechtenstein

47. Marshall Islands

48. Mexico

49. Micronesia

50. Moldova

51. Monaco

52. Montserrat (UK)

53. Morocco

54. Nauru

55. New Caledonia (France)

56. New Zealand

57. Niue (New Zealand)

58. Norfolk Island (Australia)

59. Northern Mariana Islands (USA)

60. Norway

61. Palau

62. Panama

63. Papua New Guinea

64. Paraguay

65. Peru

66. Pitcairn Islands (UK)

67. Puerto Rico (USA)

68. Saint Barthelemy

69. Saint Helena, Ascension, and Tristan da Cunha (UK)

70. Saint Kitts and Nevis

71. Saint Lucia

72. Saint Martin

73. Saint Pierre and Miquelon (France)

74. Saint Vincent and the Grenadines

75. Samoa

76. San Marino

77. Sint Maarten (Netherlands)

78. Solomon Islands

79. Suriname

80. Switzerland

81. Tokelau (New Zealand)

82. Trinidad and Tobago

83. Turks and Caicos Islands (UK)

84. Tuvalu

85. United States Virgin Islands (USA)

86. Uruguay

87. Vanuatu

88. Vatican City

89. Wallis and Futuna (France)

Countries Banned from Using Paxful

If you are from the following countries listed below, then you are not allowed to use Paxful for Bitcoin trading due to OFAC sanctions placed on the countries by the USA government.

Office of Foreign Assets Control ("OFAC") is a division of the US Department of the Treasury that administers and enforces economic and trade sanctions based on US foreign policy and national security goals against targeted foreign countries and regimes, terrorists, international narcotics traffickers, those engaged in activities related to the proliferation of weapons of mass destruction, and other threats to the national security, foreign policy, or economy of the United States.

Since Paxful is a US company, it must comply with OFAC regulations.

- Burundi
- Central African Republic Sanctions
- Cuba
- Crimea region
- Iran
- Iraq
- Lebanon

- Libya
- North Korea
- Somalia
- South Sudan-related Sanctions
- Sudan and Darfur
- Syria
- Venezuela
- Yemen

Bitcoin Trading on Paxful

Bitcoin Trading Precautions

It is vital that you are aware of basic trading tips and precautions highlighted below to avoid getting into disputes. Because if you lose a dispute, there is nowhere to protest. Not even a lawyer can save you. Your hard-earned cash will be gone, and you will be left ranting on social media.

According to Paxful CEO Rat Youssef, "If *you have ever had a dispute on Paxful you usually had to wait 20–60 minutes before it is solved, but now it can be days to a week. Right now, we have thousands of disputes open and this number has been growing daily. Our dispute moderators are drowning in gift card disputes which make up 90% of our total dispute volume and over 99.99% of the time our moderators spend on disputes*".

Therefore, it is important that you do a background check of the trader before engaging in any trade to avoid joining the dispute queue. Below are precautions and tips to consider before you start trading.

General Precautions

Diversify: Do not keep a lot of Bitcoins in one exchange platform, try to distribute them across multiple platforms. That way if you are suspended from one platform, you will not lose everything. Transferring Bitcoins from one wallet to another is simple. However, you should take note of the transaction fee so that it does not eat too much into your profits

Bulk Deposit: Do not deposit too many Bitcoins into one wallet in one go (at once). Some platforms may mark the transaction as suspicious and either lock or suspend your account. And in most of the Bitcoin exchange platforms, if you deposit too many Bitcoins without indicating a verifiable source of your Bitcoins, then you will be accused of money laundering and your Bitcoins will be locked forever. You will not be able to access your account nor withdraw them.

Paxful Terms: We have already mentioned this, but it is important to emphasize that go through the Terms of service first before you start to trade on any Bitcoin exchange platform. By so doing, you will understand the rules of the game and you will hardly be on the wrong side.

Avoid Chargebacks: Avoid chargebacks at all cost unless you have nothing to lose if your account is banned. If a chargeback occurs through a bank error (by accident) or intentional, your account will be suspended for 365 days, during which time you will not have access to your funds. It does not matter whether you have solved the dispute amicably with the affected party or not. An appeal is not possible and further inquiries into a chargeback are not addressed. After 365 days of account suspension, you will be required to verify your account and if you fail to provide all the documents required to verify your account then you will be permanently banned from the platform.

Forbidden Country: If you are on the list of forbidden countries on Paxful kindly do not waste your time creating an account. Using a VPN will help you bypass restrictions in the short term, but your account will be frozen when you least expect, and you will lose your hard-earned Bitcoins. Conform to their rules and look for another Bitcoin exchange platform that accepts traders from your country.

Open a bank dedicated to Bitcoin selling: Bitcoin trading is risky because some people use it for criminal or illegal activities like money laundering. And in some countries, cryptocurrency trading is illegal. Therefore, some banks do not want clients with accounts involved in Bitcoin Trading.

So, it is safer to open a bank account used solely for Bitcoin selling. If that account is suspended, you will be left with other accounts as you follow up on the withdrawal of funds for the suspended account. You do not want a situation where your only bank account is suspended, and you are not able to pay your bills.

Using Personal bank accounts for business transactions: For most banks, it is against their terms of operation to use a personal account for business transactions. Personal accounts are limited to personal transactions. Therefore, if you have people sending money to you, then it is advisable that they should do it from their personal accounts.

In your offer terms, indicate that buyers or sellers should only transfer money from their personal account and their bank account name should match the names in their official government ID.

Browser Malware: Your browser might be affected by malware that hijacks it and steals your Bitcoins. How it works is that when you send Bitcoins to **X address** the malware replaces your destination address (**X address**) with their address. Once Bitcoins have been sent, they cannot be reversed.

It is important to use a quality antivirus software that automatically scans and stops any malware from installing into your browser without your permission. Also, try to avoid running freeware programs, which upon installation may unpack software you are unaware of. And be sure to always keep your browser updated.

Account Level precautions

- **Blocking**: You should check how many people a trader is blocking or how many people are blocking him. A very high number of blocked users should be a cause of alarm.
- **Feedback:** You should check the feedback page of a trader to find out what people who have previously traded with the trader are saying about him or her. A very high number of negative comments about the trader should be a cause of concern.
- **Verified ID:** You should only buy from sellers with a verified ID. A verified profile is

proof that you are dealing with a person with a known identity by Paxful.

- **Active/Online:** Send "Hi" to check whether the vendor is online and responds to your message before making any payment. Cancel the trade and do not make payment if the seller is inactive or unresponsive.

- **Seller Terms**: Read through the seller's terms and make sure that you 100% agree with his or her terms. If you overlook any word in the seller's terms, then it might end up working against you if a dispute arises. Paxful gives the seller's written terms prominence when ruling on disputes. For example, when paying with PayPal a seller may indicate in the terms *"Indicate that you are sending to family and friends."* If you fail to indicate so when making your payment, then you will have yourself to blame.

- **Do not believe in word-of-mouth evidence:** Never believe in what someone is telling you, double-check and only make decisions based on solid evidence and facts. *For example, a trader telling you to release Bitcoins insisting that they have made payment before you have confirmed that the payment has arrived in your account.*

- **Record Transactions:** Always Screenshot your transaction details, download invoices, and store them in a secure place for 7 days to 12 months. You might need them just in case a dispute arises. Dispute response with evidence is most powerful when backed with supporting documents.

- **Do not hurry:** Take your time, do not be rushed, or rush other people. The first red flag is a trader who hurries you up.

- **Payment Method:** Do not sell Bitcoin using payment methods that are not permitted or allowed on Paxful. If you ignore this warning, then be aware that Paxful will not help you if you lose your money.

- **Canceling Trades:** Do not cancel a trade after payment even if a seller has asked you to do so. After paying, immediately proceed to click paid. Open a dispute if the seller is asking you to cancel a trade after paying. If you listen to the seller and go-ahead to cancel the trade, then the seller will receive back his Bitcoins and walk away with your money.

- **Releasing Bitcoins**: Never release Bitcoins before you confirm that you have received the money in your wallet. Do not believe in words like, "I have sent you money release". CONFIRM receipt.

- **Profile Age:** Consider profile age but this does not mean that old profiles cannot defraud you. Accounts can be bought or hacked. But old is better than new considering all possible security checks.

- **Using VPN to access Paxful:** Do not use a VPN to access Paxful. Some VPNs do not have a dedicated IP and may provide you with an IP from one of the Office of Foreign Assets Control (OFAC) sanctioned countries or regions. Your account will be immediately frozen or banned if you access Paxful from OFAC sanctioned country.

- **PayPal Transactions:** Be careful when dealing with people who pay you with PayPal transactions marked as "Goods and Services." PayPal transactions under goods and services are under PayPal buy protection and can easily be reversed.

- **Gift Cards:** Be careful when trading with Gift Cards. Some fraudulent sellers can redeem your gift card and claim that you sent him a used gift card, or some buyer can send you a used gift card and claim that you redeemed it. The challenge with this is that it could be hard for Paxful to judge who is wrong because they cannot know who redeemed the gift card. There are lots of scam stories to do with trading with gift cards on Paxful. Therefore, anybody in their right mind should accept or use Gift Cards as a last resort or after due diligence. The only exception where you should accept Gift Cards is when they are paid in cash as explained below.

- **Buying Verified Accounts:** Do not buy Paxful accounts. It is against their terms. If you are found to be using a bought account then it will be banned, and you will lose all your Bitcoins.

- **Multiple accounts:** Unless expressly authorized by Paxful, you are only allowed to have one account. You are not allowed to create another account if you have been previously suspended

- **Language**: Trader should be able to communicate in a language that you understand

- **Number of Trades**: Only trade with a seller who has a least 20 successful trades.

- **Trusted**: Trader should be trusted by at least 3 people

How Bitcoins move from the Seller's Account to the Buyer's Wallet on Paxful

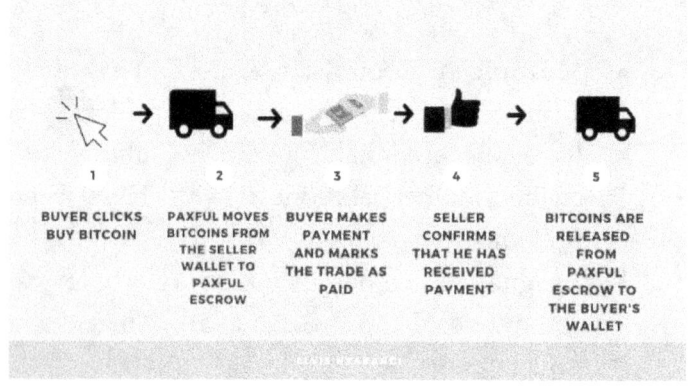

BITCOIN

MOVEMENT ON PAXFUL

1	2	3	4	5
BUYER CLICKS BUY BITCOIN	PAXFUL MOVES BITCOINS FROM THE SELLER WALLET TO PAXFUL ESCROW	BUYER MAKES PAYMENT AND MARKS THE TRADE AS PAID	SELLER CONFIRMS THAT HE HAS RECEIVED PAYMENT	BITCOINS ARE RELEASED FROM PAXFUL ESCROW TO THE BUYER'S WALLET

Once a buyer clicks Buy Bitcoins button, Paxful will immediately move the Bitcoin from the seller's wallet to Paxful Escrow account awaiting Payment. Thereafter, the buyer makes payments and marks the trade as paid.

The seller then confirms receipt of payment and clicks release Bitcoins.

The Bitcoins are then moved from Paxful's escrow account to the Buyer's wallet

If the Buyer cancels a trade after paying, before marking the trade as paid then the Bitcoins will move from Paxful escrow account to the seller's wallet. That is why it is advisable to always mark a trade as paid after making payment.

How to buy Bitcoins on Paxful

To buy Bitcoins on Paxful Marketplace follow the procedure below

1. Go to Paxful.com
2. Click on Get started
3. Log in or create an account
4. Click on Buy Bitcoin at the top menu

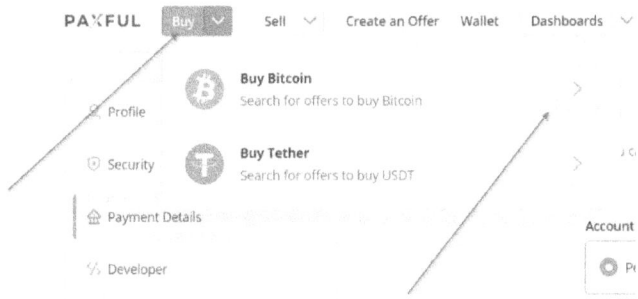

5. Select your preferred payment method and currency

6. Then enter the amount of money you want to spend in buying bitcoins.

7. Click Show Offers

8. Several offers of sellers selling Bitcoins using your Payment Method and Currency will be displayed

9. Select a seller based on the following requirements (last seen online of between just now to 4 minutes, high positive feedback, type of payment method accepted should be your preferred choice, the minimum and maximum amount they are accepting should be within your budget and exchange rate should be the best).

10. Before you click Buy button, open the seller's profile and check for some basic information to evaluate his/her credibility. Check whether the seller has a verified email, verified phone, and verified ID.

11. Once you have considered the seller credible, Click Buy.

12. Read the seller's terms carefully. Do not skip even a single word or do not proceed with buying Bitcoins if you do not agree with his or her terms. If you agree with the terms, enter the amount you want to pay and you will be able to see how many bitcoins you will receive.

13. Then Click Buy Now

14. A chat button will popup.
15. Before you pay, have a chat with the seller to ensure she/he is online or active. Agree on the payment methods. Ask for any clarifications from the seller if you have any doubts.
16. If the chat proceeds well and you agree on the payment method, then make your payment as directed by the seller.
17. Then Click Paid (If you fail to click on the Paid button after paying then the trade will timeout and the Bitcoins will return to the vendor. In a worst-case scenario you will lose your money).
18. The vendor will then confirm your payment and release the Bitcoins
19. After receiving the Bitcoins leave feedback.

If the seller does not release the Bitcoins, then the two of you (seller and buyer) should try to sort out the dispute. If the seller is not responsive or uncooperative then launch a dispute using the dispute resolution procedure below.

Selling Bitcoins on Paxful

You can sell Bitcoins on Paxful either through creating offers or directly to buyers. The two selling methods have been explained below.

Tips of Selling Bitcoins on Paxful

Price: When selling bitcoins through offers, check what competitors are offering and try to adjust your price. Targeting a very high-profit margin might lead to no profit at all or even loss if Bitcoin prices drop. When selling Bitcoins without creating an offer, consider a buyer with the best profit margins and credibility.

Negative feedback: If you are selling without creating offers, look at the buyer's feedback, avoid buyers who have the tendency of reversing payments or with chargebacks.

Terms: If you are selling without creating offers, read the buyer's terms and make sure that you agree with all his or her terms. If you overlook any word in the buyer's terms, then it might end up working against you if a dispute arises. Paxful gives the buyer's written terms prominence when ruling on disputes. Paxful terms say, *"Never submit payment unless you have followed all terms and conditions listed in the offer. If you submit payment without following the terms and conditions, Paxful cannot assist you in a dispute process to recover your payment."*

How to sell Bitcoin without creating offers

Selling Bitcoins directly by selecting a buyer of your choice is the quickest method of trading as you do not have to wait for a buyer. Just select any available buyer you prefer and sell your Bitcoins to him or her immediately. However, you are confined to the buyer's terms and requirements. Below is how to sell Bitcoins quickly.

- Login to your Bitcoin account.
- Click Sell Bitcoin.

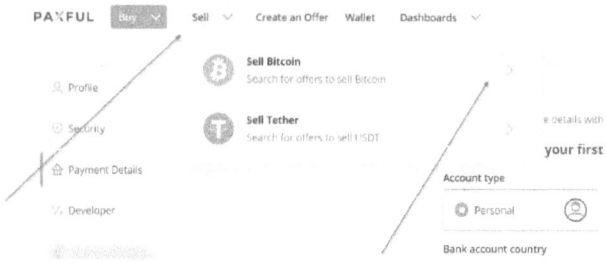

- Select your preferred payment method and Currency.
- Click Show Offers.
- Several offers of traders buying Bitcoins using your Payment Method and Currency will be displayed.
- Select a buyer based on the following requirements (last seen online of between just now to 4 minutes, high positive feedback, type of payment method accepted should be your preferred choice, the minimum and maximum amount they are accepting should be within your budget and exchange rate should be the best).
- Before you click the sell button, open the buyer's profile and check for some basic information to evaluate his/her credibility. Check whether the buyer has a verified email, verified phone, and verified ID.
- Once you have considered that the buyer is credible, Click Sell.

- Read the buyer's terms word by word. Do not proceed with selling Bitcoins if you do not agree with his or her terms. If you agree with the terms, enter the amount you want to receive and you will be able to see how many Bitcoins are required for that amount.
- Then Click Sell Now.
- A chat button will popup.
- Say "Hi" to the buyer and wait for her/him reply to confirm that she/he is online or active. Agree on the payment methods. Ask for any clarifications from the buyer if you have any doubts.
- Wait for the buyer to pay you.
- Confirm that you have received the payment in your account. Do not believe in word of mouth.
- Once you have confirmed that you have received the exact amount in your account then release the Bitcoins.
- Give the buyer a feedback and that marks the end of the trade.

How to sell Bitcoins through Creating Offers

Unlike selling Bitcoins directly by selecting a buyer, selling Bitcoins through creating offers can take time as you will have to compete with other sellers for buyer attention. However, the buyer must trade under your terms and requirements. Below is how to create offers.

- Login to your account
- Click Create an offer at the top menu bar

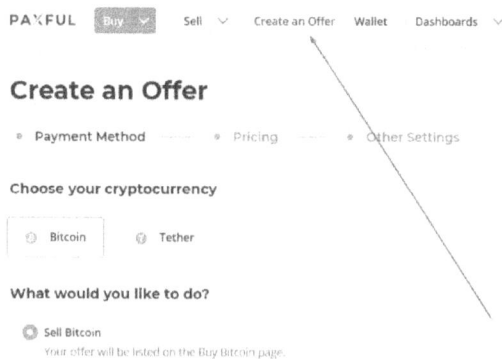

- Click Sell Bitcoin

- Select Payment Method that you accept: Use payment methods that are acceptable in your location and which are not easy to reverse.
- Select Preferred currency
- Click Next
- **Select Percent above Market rate offer** (this the percent of the profit you want to make on top of the current Bitcoin exchange rate). For example, if 1 Bitcoin=$40,000. You can set it to 10% percent and the buyer will buy it at 1B=$44,000.
- **Set offer trade limits**: This is the minimum and maximum amount of amount that the buyer should trade. Start small and grow over time.
- **Offer Limit**: The time when a trade will take before it is completed. Once the time has expired the trade will be canceled. 30 minutes is ideal
- Click Next
- **Offer Tags**: Here you are supposed to include requirements like cards only or cash only. Tags are particularly important as they will help you mitigate risks and keep away scammers. This is the first thing a buyer sees when they open a trade.
- **You offer label**: A message that will attract buyers for example BTC Released instantly, Available online 24/7

- **Offer Terms**: Explain in detail the terms that your buyers must meet before buying from you. Below are examples of Terms.
- **Trade instructions**: Just copy and paste your term to trade instructions.
- **Verification**: verified email, verified phone, and profile are not necessary. I do not recommend checking the boxes. This is because you are going to minimize your sales.
- **Target Country**: If you have specified a specific country currency and payment method then it is also advisable that you target traders from that country. For example, if you accept Mpesa payments only then it means Kenya is your ideal target country.
- Other remaining options are not necessary.
- Publish your offer if you are done.

How to Send Bitcoin to External Wallets

You can send Bitcoins to an external wallet from Paxful wallet. For instance, to Coinbase, LocalBitcoin Wallet using the procedure below.

Before you send your Bitcoins to an external wallet be aware that once you send the Bitcoins they cannot be reversed. Transaction fees of sending Bitcoins from Paxful wallet to external have been indicated above.

- Go to your wallet in your account
- Click the SEND button in your wallet.

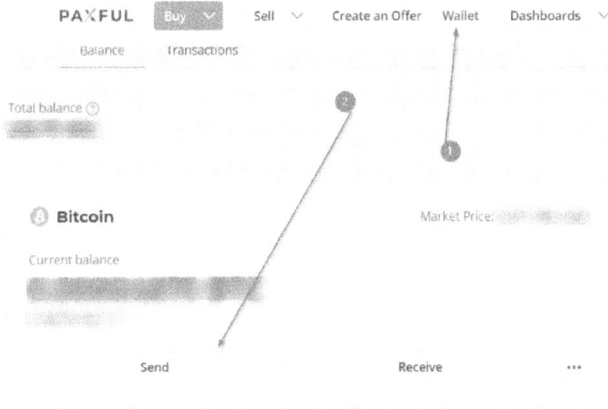

- Type in the amount you want to send in either Bitcoin or currency.
- Paste the Bitcoin address where you want to send the Bitcoins to.
- Click send and then click confirm.

Transferring Bitcoins to internal Wallets

To transfer bitcoins to another Paxful account.

- Go to your wallet in your account
- Click the SEND button in your wallet.
- Type in the amount you want to send in either Bitcoin or currency.

- Click Send to Paxful username instead
- Enter the recipient's Paxful username
- Click Continue

How to receive Bitcoins from an External Wallet

To receive Bitcoins from an external wallet, all you need is to provide your Bitcoin wallet address to the sender. Once they send the Bitcoins, they will reflect in your Paxful wallet.

- Click Wallet
- Then Click Receive Button
- You will see your wallet address in characters or QR code form
- Provide the sender your wallet address (characters) or QR code.

Trading with Gift Cards tips

Here is a simple story explained by Paxful CEO on how difficult it is to solve Gift Card disputes'

"iTunes gift cards are irreversible, much like Bitcoins, however, with Bitcoin you can easily check the balance of any account on a public ledger, with iTunes you cannot as it is a private system. This means absolute chaos when trying to award disputes. 99% of all iTunes gift card trades on Paxful go smoothly out of tens of thousands every week yet that 1% is taxing our human resources.

Our dispute moderators must spend days on each one collecting evidence from both sides. Often it comes down to a coin flip as 99% of the people who get these cards are Nigerians and they get them online through brokering, which is against the Paxful Terms of Service. This is because they have no idea if the codes, they bought are good or not thus causing massive confusion and wasting people's time, hence why we forbid brokering. You cannot check the validity of an iTunes gift card until you redeem it which makes it worthless instantly. Nigerians buy these cards through online brokering and then sell them on Paxful for Bitcoin, usually to Chinese vendors (what they do with 11 million in iTunes gift cards a week is another story). Imagine going into a trade dispute with a Nigerian person and Chinese vendor both cursing each other in their respective languages and colorful English. Is the Chinese vendor with 10,000 feedback ripping the Nigerian trader? The Nigerian iTunes gift card trader has no idea if the code he has is valid and while sometimes it is many will swear on their life that it is valid. The Chinese vendors sometimes make mistakes with card balances getting confused from many simultaneous trades but there have been confirmed cases of ripping. Our mods ask the Nigerian iTunes trader to call apple and get recorded proof of who used the card and when. Most Nigerians do not bother to call the overseas number and record the conversation, it is difficult for them, yet the burden of proof is on them to prove the value of the card. The point stands that there is no simple or quick way to get to the bottom of this."

Having read the statement from Paxful CEO himself, you understand how risky it is to deal with Gift cards. However, gift cards have high-profit margins, therefore, you may be tempted to still give them a try despite the risk. Below are precautions that you should take when exchanging Gift Cards for Bitcoins.

- **"Say Hi and wait for me to respond"**: This is to avoid people who will start trading with you when you are not online
- **Currency**: Specify the currency that you accept. For example, "US Dollar ($US) Amazon Gift Cards only"
- **Take time:** Do not accept to be hurried. Indicate to your buyers to be patient until you tell them to upload the gift card receipt photos.
- **AQ Cards:** Only accept Gift cards that start with AQ. Codes that start with AQ are physical cards.
- **Offer tags**: This is important and you should pay close attention to it. Your buyers are going to see these tags before they start trading with you. To avoid being scammed with used cards add the following tags;

  - ➢ **Physical cards only**: The buyer should send you a picture of the physical card. Do not take ecodes

> ➤ **Cash Only**: The buyer must have paid the gift card with cash. Avoid gift cards paid with credit cards.
> ➤ **Balance:** When redeeming the cards, make sure that the amount matches the trade volume.

- **Region Restriction:** Check whether the card has any region restrictions. For example "valid only in the united states".
- **Receipt:** You should ask for the payment receipt

NOTE: Every seller on Paxful who trades cryptocurrency using a gift card offer is required to upload a security deposit to ensure the safety of Paxful buyers. Security deposits can be as low as 0.005 BTC. The security deposit is for gift card trades only. For other payment types like cash, online wallets, and debit/credit cards, a security deposit is not required. If you do not have enough BTC in your account to cover the security deposit, your offer will not be activated. Your deposit amount is released 7 days after your last gift card trade.

Sample Paxful Offer Terms and what they mean

PayPal Terms

When using PayPal, always be aware that its reversibility risks are the highest. Scammers keep creating accounts which they use for scamming and then throw them away. It appears that the cycle of creating accounts, scamming, discarding, and creating news ones again will never end any time soon. Even if you are dealing with an extremely trusted trader, observe these precautions and terms.

- **User must use a verified PayPal account**: This is to avoid dealing with scammers who create PayPal accounts quickly for the sole purpose of scamming.
- **I do not accept funds from credit cards and debit cards through PayPal**: This is to avoid bank chargebacks. Banks are 100% guaranteed to rule in the bank account owner's favor if he files for a chargeback.
- **You must Prove that funds are available in your PayPal account**: To avoid people paying with credit or debit card via PayPal.
- **Provide a link to your Facebook Profile**: To do a background check and verify the profile of the trader you are dealing with.

63

- Send screenshot showing that funds originated from PayPal balance to avoid being paid with credit or debit card via PayPal.

- **Send to family and friends:** The seller should indicate that he/she is paying to family and friends and not goods and services. This is because PayPal does not offer refunds for payments sent using the Friends and Family functionality unless you prove that your account was compromised

- **Confirm email**: Before a buyer pays, ask him to provide you with his email and then send random numbers like 1239 and ask him to mention the numbers you have sent to his email. This is to confirm that the PayPal email address belongs to him and that he has not hacked the email address.

- **Check email for fraud:** Google the email address of the buyer and check the results that come up. If you come across any search results mentioning the email's involvement in any fraudulent activity, then avoid the trade.

Sample Interac e-transfer Terms

- **Upload a clear picture of your Canadian Government-issued ID**: This is to verify your identity and nationality
- **A video of you holding your ID while mentioning the Bitcoin seller's name**: This to confirm that you are the real owner of the ID and the video was taken at the time of the trade (not pre-recorded)

Sample Cash in person terms

- **Time**: Indicate the time that you are available for a trade for example 9:00 AM to 4:00 PM.
- **Location**: Indicate the exact building and office number where you are located
- **SMS alert when coming**: Trader should alert you via SMS when coming to your office to avoid missing you
- **Do not click Paid before handing me cash**: Trader must visit your office and hand you the cash before they click the paid button. A receipt will be issued after making payment.
- **Payment Type**: Indicate the payment method that you do not accept.

Sample Bank Transfer

Send a photo of your ID that you used to register your bank account: This is to verify that account details are the same as registered ID details.

Common Paxful scams and how to avoid them

In cryptocurrency trading, scammers are everywhere. They take pride in the fact that Cryptocurrencies are unregulated in most countries and nothing will happen to them if they scam you. Below are common Paxful scams.

Scam 1: Trader reversing payment after release of Bitcoins

Case: *"I am a newbie on Paxful. Please be careful before you start trading on Paxful, especially if you trade with Neteller, Skrill, Payoneer, and similar payment methods.*

I have already lost my money with Neteller, Skrill, and Payoneer trader. Some dishonest trader issued a payment with their self-account, after the trade was completed the trader made a claim to Skrill for reversal of funds claiming that someone hacked their account and transferred money out.

Another case happened where a trader hacked someone's account and used the hacked account to make payment. The account owner then later regained his account and asked for fund reversal.

Because most online payment processing companies do not support Bitcoin exchange, your account will end up being locked and you will lose your Bitcoins.

I can't blame Skrill, Neteller, or Payoneer because they don't support Bitcoin exchange."

Solution: The buyer should provide you a photo of their National ID to confirm that the account they are paying you with belongs to them and is not a case of hacking. Also make sure that you have withdrawn your money from Skrill, Payoneer as soon as it is issued before releasing Bitcoins.

Scam 2: Paying with stolen credit cards

Case: The way this scam works is that scammers usually get access to hacked or fraudulent bank accounts or credit cards and then purchase large amounts of crypto currencies. They will then either transfer the Bitcoins to a different online wallet or personal wallets to avoid being tracked or losing their Bitcoins if you file a dispute on Paxful.

What happens later is that the Bitcoin seller who was paid with stolen credit cards will get a chargeback or have his bank account suspended for fraudulent activity. In this case, the seller will lose his money and Bitcoins.

Solution: Ask for a National ID to verify that the name on the credit card is the same as the one on the National ID. Also, trade with verified users only and never accept third-party bank transactions.

Scam 3: man-in-the-middle scam

Case: This type of scam in Bitcoin trading happens this way.

1. Scammer pretends to be selling Bitcoins for **10K** dollars and finds a buyer, **John**.

2. Scammer contacts **you** and agrees to buy Bitcoins for **10K** dollars.

3. Scammer tells John to send **10K** dollars to your bank account.

4. You receive **10K** dollars from John and you release the Bitcoins to the Scammer.

5. Scammer transfers Bitcoins to his external wallet and disappears into thin air.

6. John does not receive his Bitcoins and decides to ask for a refund from his payment processor.

7. John gets a chargeback

8. You lose your Bitcoin, and you are put under investigation by your bank

Solution: Ask for a photo of the government ID that matches the buyer's bank account and check the source of funds before releasing Bitcoins

Dispute resolution process on Paxful

You have just been scammed or are about to be scammed or you need help solving a trade dispute. Below is how to go about it. If a seller is unresponsive and you have not made payment then cancel the trade.

Dispute resolution for Bitcoin Buyers

1. To start a dispute, Go to the trade page
2. Click the Dispute button (*the button will only appear once you have marked the transaction as paid*).

YOU PAID 15 US DOLLARS WITH BANK TRANSFER.
PLEASE WAIT FOR THE VENDOR TO RELEASE
BITCOINS TO YOUR WALLET

13.4 US Dollars will be loaded to your bitcoin wallet

3. Select the topic of your dispute (Unresponsive vendor, Coinlocker, etc).

4. Provide sufficient information with supporting evidence on why you are starting a dispute

5. Then click the start dispute button

6. A moderator will join the chat discussion

7. Provide as many details as possible with documents to support your case. Examples of documents that you can provide to support your case include, screenshots of the trade, proof of payment, invoice or bill, bank statement, cash receipt, etc.). However, do not provide sensitive information like Credit Card expiry date and security code.

8. Once you have provided your evidence then be patient and wait for the Paxful dispute resolution team to review your case.

9. If you followed the seller's terms and provided all the required documentation

within the required time, then be sure that you will win the case.

Dispute resolution for Bitcoin sellers.

1. Go to Trader Partners (below your profile image on desktop/pc/laptop)

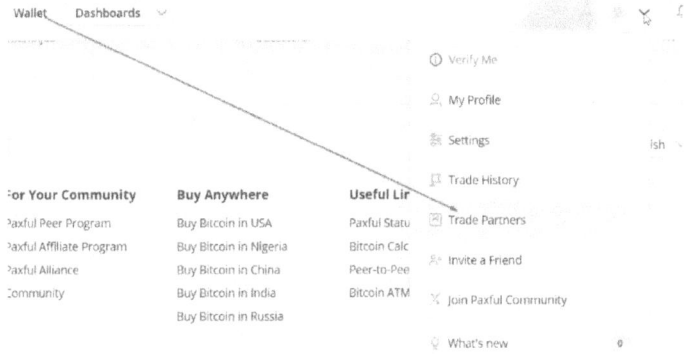

2. *On recent trades page, click on the three continuous dots on the right of the trader you have a problem with.*
3. Click view this trade
4. Scroll to the bottom and click report a problem

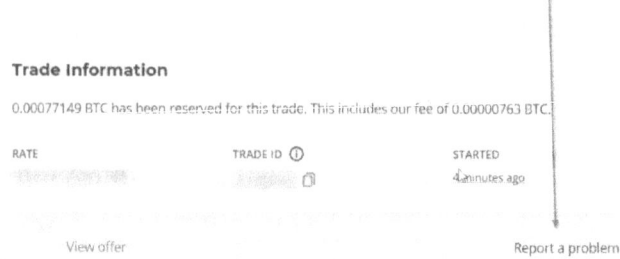

Trade Information

0.00077149 BTC has been reserved for this trade. This includes our fee of 0.00000763 BTC.

RATE	TRADE ID ⓘ	STARTED
		4 minutes ago

View offer   Report a problem

5. Select what you are reporting for (Abusive Language, Used Gift Card Code, Impersonating moderator, chargeback, or other)
6. Enter Description of the problem and click report

Lost Dispute: Paxful terms state that, "*If you believe Paxful has resolved a dispute in a way which is not in accordance with this Agreement, you have a right to request an appeal. To request an appeal, you need to promptly notify us in writing by contacting Paxful customer support no later than 10 calendar days after notice of Paxful Support's decision is delivered to you and provide us with sufficient details and evidence supporting your case for request. Your appeal should specifically identify how you believe Paxful incorrectly resolved the dispute as per the terms of this Agreement and provide evidence of such incorrect decision.*"

How to Contact Paxful

There are different methods that you can use to contact Paxful support team.

Support through Email Contacts

You can contact Paxful via email using the following contacts.

- **Help**: help@paxful.zendesk.com
- **Press coverage**: press@paxful.com
- **Account Security**: security@paxful.com

Support through Dashboard Account

To get support through your dashboard, Open the trade dispute **as shown above** and select any of the available reporting options.

- **Report a Problem:** Report any problem that you are facing on that trade
- **Report Chargeback**: Report trader who has made a chargeback
- **Report a scam**: report a trader who has scammed you.
- Report a problem if you have not been paid and you have released Bitcoins

Support through Social Media

You can contact Paxful on social media through the following channels

- **Paxful on twitter**: You can reach Paxful on twitter through https://twitter.com/paxful
- **Paxful on Facebook**: You can message Paxful on Facebook through https://www.facebook.com/paxful
- **Paxful on Reddit**: This is the best place if you are a newbie, and you need support not only from Paxful but other community members: https://www.reddit.com/r/paxful/, you can also tag Martha: https://www.reddit.com/user/Martha_Paxful who is one of Paxful support team for a quick response.
- **Paxful on Telegram**: USA (https://t.me/paxful_usa_community), India (https://t.me/paxful_indian_community), Kenya (https://t.me/paxful_kenyan_community), South Africa (https://t.me/paxfulsouthafricancommunity), Nigeria (https://t.me/paxful_nigerian_community), Ghana (https://t.me/paxful_ghanaian_community),

More telegram communities
(https://paxful.com/community)

Support through forms

- **Google form:** If you have previously contacted Paxful and you have not heard from them in days, then you can escalate your issue through this form: https://docs.google.com/forms/d/e/1FAIpQLSdjONom3sE-UT3XYQpQ0Nj0naSxLU3Uh2zTkgMzRZLqJBVCjQ/viewform **or use short link** https://rb.gy/jd0gp2

Mailing Address

- You can mail Paxful through 3422 Old Capitol Trail #989, Wilmington, DE, United States

Paxful Physical Location

Paxful is registered as Paxful Holdings, New York, United States. Its business address is.

- Street 1: 44 W. 28th Street

- Street 2: 5th Floor

- City: New York

Phone Number

- Paxful's official registered business phone number is: 917-609-3850

Conclusion

Bitcoin emerged from the 2008 financial crisis and has grown to be the world's first and largest decentralized cryptocurrency. It is hailed by cryptocurrency fanatics as a liberator and vilified by critics as a safe haven for criminals.

There are other cryptocurrencies that have existed before Bitcoin. But what makes Bitcoin unique is that it is decentralized. It came to solve the problem of intermediaries.

Why the need for Bitcoin Exchange platforms?

The main reason why Bitcoin exchange platforms like Paxful exist is to help people convert their mined Bitcoins into real money (legal currency) like Euros, Dollars, Yen, Pound, etc. For instance, you can transfer your Bitcoins to your Paxful wallet and then sell them in exchange for dollars that will be transferred to your bank or payment processor.

Once banks and payment processing companies legally begin accepting Bitcoins as a means of exchange, then Bitcoin exchange platforms like Paxful will only act as bitcoin trading platforms just as it is to forex trading platforms.

Future of Bitcoin

Bitcoin came and grew too fast before regulations were put in place on how it operates. Countries have begun passing laws in favor and others against Bitcoins use by their citizens. 20 years from now, we should expect that all countries would have put in place regulations on Bitcoin use. The benefit of having regulations is that they will help accelerate the adoption of Bitcoin as a means of payment by commercial entities.

Below are examples of fortune 100 companies that have announced that they will adopt Bitcoin which provides every indication that the future looks good for Bitcoin investors.

- Paypal announced that in 2021, its users will be allowed to buy, sell and hold select Cryptocurrencies directly through PayPal using their Cash or Cash Plus account.
- On February 10th, 2021, MasterCard announced that it will be accepting cryptocurrencies in its network to prepare for the future.
- In a filing with the SEC, Tesla, Inc. announced that it had bought Bitcoins worth $1.5 billion

My Bitcoin Trading Experience

I have traded Bitcoins on Paxful for over 3 years and I have never been scammed nor made any loss.

Over the 3 years of my trading, I have always treated Bitcoin trading on Paxful as a business with the potential of high returns and high risks. It might seem scary but adopting a cautious mindset has been immensely helpful to me. It has made me more watchful, careful, and sensitive to details than I have ever been in other businesses that I have invested in. And in return, I have never lost a cent to scammers. What does this mean for you?

Trading Bitcoins on Paxful is risky because there are thousands of scammers there waiting for newbies to scam, however, if you observe all the tips provided in this book, you can turn Bitcoin trading into a profitable source of income.

When it comes to the ideal payment method, the rule of thumb is that you should never deal with reversible payment methods like PayPal, Skrill, and Credit Cards, even if a trader provides adequate documents to prove that they are the real owners of the account. Documents can be generated online or tampered with and criminals know how to create them in a manner that makes them look original to the untrained eye.

Only use reversible payment methods if you are dealing with extremely trusted traders.

Should you invest in Bitcoin?

Investing in Bitcoin has been a hot topic among investors around the Globe. Which is why learning how to invest in Bitcoin using the right information is important. Is Bitcoin a worthwhile investment?

The major disadvantage that exists with the use of Bitcoin is its volatile nature. Before you decide whether you should adopt it or not for your business, you have to be mentally and financially prepared that it could crash anytime.

For now, the only advice is to start small, invest in what you can afford to lose.

Bitcoin Risk warning!

Bitcoin is considered volatile because of how much and how quickly its value can change. Like any other currency, there is a potential for gains and losses.

Learning Resources

Below are a few websites to keep yourself informed about Bitcoin developments.

- **BitcoinTalk.org**: The largest Bitcoin forum where you can get updated and experiences of people trading Bitcoin
- **Bitcoin on Reddit**: The largest Bitcoin community with over 2.4 million members sharing their thoughts and tips about Bitcoin (https://www.reddit.com/r/Bitcoin/)
- **Bitcoin.org**: A Bitcoin resource website
- **Bitcoin Resources for beginners** (https://www.lopp.net/bitcoin-information.html)
- **Explain Bitcoin Like I'm Five**: An article that simplifies the question of what is Bitcoin? (https://medium.com/free-code-camp/explain-bitcoin-like-im-five-73b4257ac833)

About the Author

Elvis was born in Nairobi, Kenya. He holds a Bachelor of Arts degree in Linguistics, Media, and Communication from Moi University. He has been involved in Bitcoin since 2016. He is the founder and owner of Kyote Internet Group Limited, a company that invests in digital technologies.